Dale Earr

Jr.

The Legend of Dale Earnhardt

Jr.

By Naven Johnson

Copyright © 2019 by Naven Johnson

All rights reserved. This book or any portion thereof may not be reproduced or used in any manner whatsoever without the express written permission of the publisher except for the use of brief quotations in a book review.

Printed in the United States of America

First Printing, 2019

Table of Contents

Chapter 1 5

Chapter 2 7

Chapter 3 11

Chapter 4 14

Chapter 5 16

Chapter 6 23

Chapter 7 28

Chapter 1
The Origin

From a German ancestral race, Earnhardt was born to the family of Dale Earnhardt and Brenda Lorraine in the city of Kannapolis North Carolina. Luckily, Earnhardt's family had a background in NASCAR as his mother's father was a car maker for NASCAR. He had quite a lot of siblings as his father had a previous marriage before getting married to his mother, and a third marriage after divorcing his mother.

Kelly was his sister; Kerry was his half-brother from the first marriage, while Taylor was his half-sister from the third marriage. He and his sister Kelly lived with their mother Brenda until he was six years old. At this time, Brenda lacked a positive financial source as a result of her house having been ravaged by fire and had to give up the custody of the children to her ex-husband. At the age of 12 his father enrolled him in a military school. After graduation he got his start in racing.

During this time, he competed on the South and North Carolina short tracks with his Chevrolet. Despite the short tracks he participated in, Earnhardt was more focused on the Myrtle Beach Speedway in the East and South Carolina Motor Speedway in Robertsonville North Carolina. On the 28th of October 1994, he won the Greenville Merchant 300. This is where he learned car preparation and chassis setup while racing his siblings. He bagged a degree in automotive technology at the Mitchell Community College.

Chapter 2
Dale's Business Life

Having a successful business career alongside his sporting career is one that deserves a lot of accolades. Dale definitively earned a lot of money as a car racer. This alone could make one so relaxed when it came to making more money, but that was not the case for Dale. He was smart enough to understand that times were likely coming when he would be unable to race, which would mean no money for him. Dale's sister and advisor Kelly noted that he capitalized on the popularity he earned as a sportsman to bolster his business career. She stated expressly that he has had the best opportunity to thrive in the business world.

Of recent, Earnhardt was named the highest paid driver in NASCAR consecutively for the fifth time with about 25 million USD on the average both from his share in both wins and salary. More so, he is said to earn about 13 million USD from endorsements outside the track as he was a partner to organizations like Goody's, Chevrolet, etc.

He is known for his business philosophy of aligning with the right set of individuals, being authentic at every point in time, never overthinking, and always having fun. Undoubtedly, his philosophical approach and his fan base are reasons why he is thriving business wise. The truth is this approach wasn't what he started with.

He had not always thought or seen a diversified portfolio as one beyond sport. He rather saw it centering around the number of victories he could accumulate on the track. All he wanted to do was to win as much as possible and enjoy victory for the next 15-20 years.

However, he reneged on those thoughts after his fifth season of the sprint cup. He developed the feeling that he was already an established driver with a rich portfolio in the racing history and at that point in time, he was enjoying his best season with sixteen tops-5 finishes, 6 wins, and a 5th place. He became matured in his thinking and began to dabble into the business world.

His business career started off with him saving some of his money in the bank and in the stock exchange market. However, it was a very slow progressive run until he got a car dealership opportunity with partners like Rick Hendrick. He also partnered with Bob Durkin in the bar and restaurant business. He had a special interest in the car dealership, and he took ample time to study and get accustomed to its intricacies, visiting it as often as time permitted.

It was revealed by Miller that Dale has one bar in Jacksonville, Fla, another in Charlotte, N.C, and a third one, still undergoing construction, in Long Island, New York. All are said to be very lucrative. Dale confessed that they are a good source of income and even compared the income he gets from these businesses with that which he earns as a race car driver. He categorically stated at one time that they are just as important and lucrative as racing.

Dale said he still has not gotten a clear view of the total picture, but he is certain that with time, he will. This is why he made the decision to prepare for the time when he would not be driving any longer. "After driving, what is next?", he asked. He said he chose the car dealership business because it is something he can engage in until he is about 70 years old. Earnhardt's manager, Mr. Miller, claims to be astounded by his business career. Miller believes that Earnhardt became more mature as he became more involved with business.

Chapter 3
Earnhardt Entertainment and Gaming Career

Earnhardt did not stop with the dealership and bar business. He went ahead to establish a television production firm known as Hammerhead Ent. alongside JR Motorsports, which is a nationwide series team. The good thing about these business ventures is that he is creating employment opportunities for a lot of people.

Currently, there are 5 people employed on a full-time basis and 2 people on a part-time basis in his Television Production firm. There are another 75 personnel working full time in JR Motorsports. Here, 40 work on cars while the other 35 work in departments like IT, marketing, accounting, transportation, and the facility department.

It was smart for him to establish Hammerhead since the TV commercials he features in are usually produced by his production firm, and also stands as a platform for other sponsors. Farmers Insurance, Sprint, Ingersoll-Rand and many other firms are major clients of Dale's entertainment company.

One edge Dale has had over others in the racing game is his popularity. For 10 consecutive years, Dale has been voted as the most popular NASCAR driver and as a result, he has been featured on numerous TV promotions and commercials. For his business, he has remained the face and brand ambassador.

Recently, Sprint hired him to promote an application known as "Drive First" which helps drivers detect any movement above 10 mph. Once detected, the application puts the phone on a lockdown, preventing calling and texting. However, an automated message is sent to the caller that the recipient is driving and would be unable to pick up until later.

Dale was more than glad to be a part of it. He regarded himself as a good messenger sent to do the work of God. You shouldn't be surprised if told after numerous commercials and promotions that Dale was a wonderful actor. His expression, tone, smile and grin were all perfect. Vincent Scott, a director for Sprint, regarded him as very flexible. Vincent noted that Dale could get an acting scene completed in less than half of the time it usually takes.

Chapter 4
Earnhardt's Chips

Without relenting, Dale went ahead to venture into producing potato chips under the umbrella of Dale Jr. Foods. This came into being by partnering with KLN Family Brands. This partnership birthed four flavors of potato chips: Caroline Barbecue, Crispy Original, Creole & Green Onion and Zesty Jalapeno.

Dale was instrumental in the selection of these flavors as he made the final decision from 15 different flavors. He claims that it is not so much the money that can be realized, but more the fact that it is fun for him. He said at a point that he is well aware of the fact that fun should not be the primary motive to venture into business, but that's how he feels and as long as the fans are enjoying it, it's good for him.

There is a claim by Miller that Earnhardt gets about 3 to 4 business advances every week. Earnhardt claims that the business ideas he gets are usually not planned, but due to his popularity a lot of businesses come knocking on his door. While there are a lot of opportunities, Dale believes you cannot just jump on every one of those ideas. He believes that every business he chooses to engage in has to be one that suits his personality, which would help create a strong bond with his customers.

Dale was also a part of an investment group which was saddled with the responsibility of building Alabama Motorsports. He opened one Whiskey River Bar in Charlotte, another in Jacksonville, and has an eye frame brand in addition to being and automobile dealer.

Chapter 5
Earnhardt's Racing Career

In the year 2000, Earnhardt had his breakthrough in the cup series. He was among the competitors for the Raybestos Award for the rookie of the year that same year. Matt Kenseth was another competitor for the award and was a major opponent to Earnhardt as he beat Earnhardt in the Daytona-500. Meanwhile, Earnhardt recorded his initial win at Texas Motor Speedway in the DirecTV 500, beating his father's record for having the least amount of starts in modern NASCAR when he won the competition in his twelfth start. He also repeated this feat in the Richmond International Raceway. Also, Earnhardt became the first person to win The Winston as a Rookie.

At the Winston Cup 2000, Earnhardt was part of another achievement as he competed with his stepbrother and father at the Michigan International Speedway in the Pepsi 400. This event was the second in history where a father competed with his sons on the track. The first record was when Lee Petty competed with Maurice and Richard Petty.

At the end of 2000, Earnhardt had 2 wins, 5 top 10s, 3 top 5s, and 2 poles. The year 2001 was a terrible one for Earnhardt at first. February 18 hosted one of the most important competitions of the season, the Daytona 500. Earnhardt and Michael Waltrip, his teammate, finished 2nd and 1st respectively. Meanwhile, Dale's father had crashed in the fourth turn after Sterling Marlin hit him. As a result, he developed a basilar skull fracture which eventually led to his death.

Afterward, he was declared the winner of the EA Sports 500 after a crash had happened at Talladega. Bobby Labonte flipped and crashed into 15 other cars behind Dale. As a result of this win, Earnhardt earned a Winston

Bull 5 and a one-million-dollar bonus. He later went on to win 4 restrictor plate races that year, finishing with 3 wins, fifteen top 10s, nine top 5s, and 2 poles.

2002 was not the best year for Dale either. He had much to endure after suffering from a concussion after a collision with the outer wall in April at a California race. He complicated the whole issue by failing to admit this injury until sometime around September. After California, he did not exceed above the 30th position on the table, but managed to win the two Talladega races, a Bull Pole award for 11th position, in addition to sixteen top ten and eleven top five finishes.

2003 was a better year as he was a force to reckon with. He won the Talladega race for the fourth time in a row despite being involved in a crash with about 27 cars on the fourth lap. After the crash, Dale managed to get back on track, struggling to win. In fact, a lot of controversies were raised after he was pronounced winner as he was said to have crossed the yellow boundary to win.

NASCAR defended their decision by stating Matt Kenseth forced him into the position, so it didn't count against Dale. Afterward, in October he was victorious at Phoenix, bagging him a record-breaking third position in the standings with 21 top 10s and 13 top 5 finishes. He bagged the Most Popular Driver Award by NMPA for the first time.

2004 saw Earnhardt win the Daytona 500. He almost won the speed week, but did win the Gatorade duel, Busch series, and bagged the second position in the Budweiser Shootout. He went on to be an outstanding car owner as in 2005 he and his team won the USAR Hooters Pro Cup series once and qualified for the 4th championship playoff.

2006 came, and during the Talladega Superspeedway, the DEI drivers honored Earnhardt's late father by driving with painted schemes on their cars. Earnhardt also used a Budweiser car on fathers' day to honor his grandfather and father at the Michigan International Speedway.

Although the race ended abruptly due to the wet track condition, Earnhardt finished third.

The 2006 season was a good one for him as he finished third in the standings after racing 17 times. In the same 2006 season, Dale experienced his 2nd engine failure at the New Hampshire race. This event allowed him a 43rd finish.

Next there was the Pocono race of which he crashed in the second turn. The New Hampshire race and the Pocono race cost him his position in the standings as he dropped to 11th from 3rd position. Afterwards, he and his teammates resolved to fight harder in the Indianapolis Motor Speedway in order to ensure that they were among the top 10. They did well and almost won first place for the race at Talladega until he was displaced in the last lap by a collision with his teammate Jimmie Johnson. As such, Brian Vickers ended up winning. In the end, Dale finished 5th.

In 2007, he started the NASCAR Nextel Cup Series by securing the 32nd position at the Daytona 500. This loss was due to a car crash he had during the race. Then he earned a better achievement by finishing 7th in the Food City 500 at the Bristol Motor Speedway as a result, he finished among the top 10. He later joined the league of the top 5 by leading 136 laps and finishing 5th in the Goody's Cool Orange 500.

His performance at the 2007 Aaron's 499 gave him his 3rd top 10 of the season and his 8th overall at the Talladega Super Speedway where he finished in 7th place. May 14th, 2007 left him docked of a hundred championship points. Teresa, the car owner, was docked a hundred owner points while the chief of his crew paid a fine of $100k. He was then suspended for the next six races because of the implementation of mounting brackets which were deemed to be illegal.

At the Pocono race on the 5th of August 2007, Dale for the first time earned the first pole position of his career since 2002. While Busch went ahead to win the race, Earnhardt had a spectacular comeback and ended up second. Busch took over the lead after Earnhardt had dominated 8 laps. At the Glen, Dale tried to make a top 12 only to have his engine develop some difficulties after getting to the second position.

That day, he had to pull out of the race. He still did not give up afterwards, but a duo effect of Busch and a bad engine ended his dreams of getting into the top 12. This ended his time with Dale Earnhardt Inc. as he moved on to another company. He went on to win the NMPA most popular driver for the 5th time.

Chapter 6
Dale and Hendrick Motorsport

There had been a lot of controversies as to whether Dale would leave DEI or not. DEI is a company founded by his father, and he had always driven for them ever since its inception. However, Dale decided to leave on the 10th of May 2007 to join another racing team.

He backed up his desire to leave by stating expressly that he needs to leave to achieve his dreams of being a Sprint Cup champion. He stated that he would be unable to achieve his dreams with DEI unless he gains major ownership and control of the company. He lacked confidence in the company's ability to provide the necessary equipment needed to win the Sprint Cup Championship.

On the 13th of June 2017, Dale signed a contract of five years with Hendrick Motorsports and replaced Kyle Busch. At that time, Hendrick racers were Jeff Gordon, Jimmie Johnson, and Casey Mears. A month later his sponsor Budweiser showed great concern against his move to Hendrick and pulled out of sponsoring him.

Later, on the 15th of August, he was denied access to take his accustomed no. 8 trademark. Both his grandfather and father had used the number at some points in their career and Dale wanted to retain it. He claimed he was not allowed to retain it because his stepmother hindered him, asking for the licensing revenue and a return of the number after Dale Sr. had retired. Unfortunately, after the success the No. 8 team enjoyed in 2008, they did not progress into 2009 as DEI merged with Ganassi Racing.

Tony Eury Jr. remained his crew chief at Hendrick as Dale was given the No. 88 car to Drive. Fortunately, NASCAR history has it that the No 88 was once driven by Ralph Earnhardt, Dale's grandfather, in the year 1957. Robert Gee, his maternal grandfather is also said to have a history with Hendrick Motorsports. Hendrick went on to merge with Earnhardt's Motorsport as the cars they used came directly from Dale's shop. Good for Dale.

He won the Budweiser Shootout at the beginning of the 2008 season and it was also his first for Hendrick Motorsports. Leading 47 laps out of 70 laps and breaking the Budweiser shootout record. He complemented these five days by winning his first Gatorade duels which happened to be the 3rd duel he would win in his whole career.

His smooth run came to an end when he finished 9th in the Daytona 500. Although, he started well, due to some unforeseen circumstances, like missing a pit stop, pitting out of his pit box and a crash on the 124th lap, he finished as the 27th racer. To date, the crash remains a very controversial one.

At Las Vegas he ended up as the 10th in position and 29th in points. He also ended up with a bad engine in California, his owner's points fell to 35 and at Martinsville he finished 8th. His poor run continued as he finished 31st and 20th at Phoenix and Texas respectively.

He was able to gain confidence at Talladega along with his teammates. They led for 20 laps before finally finishing in 2nd place. He returned to his losing streak as he finished in the 27th position at Richmond and Darlington, before finishing 10th in the Lowe's Motor Speedway All-star race and 40th in the Coca-Cola 600.

The 6th of February 2010 saw Dale qualify as the second best for the fifty-second Daytona 500. He was first in the Gatorade Duel 2 and finished 11th in the Budweiser shootout as a result of a bad car. 2011 welcomed him with a 19th position and a pole draw at the Budweiser Shootout. The 13th of February saw him earn the first Daytona International Speedway pole position and it was also his first time on a track with a Receptors Plate.

At a point, Dale had to race from the back for both 500 and the duel race. At the Daytona 500, he ended up finishing in the 24th position with just four laps to go. In the 7 races afterwards, he achieved 5 top 10 finishes which included a second position at the Martinsville Speedway. He could have won if Kevin Harvick had not overtaken him with just four laps left. He also finished 7th at the coca cola 600, 2nd at Kansas and 6th at Pocono. He went down in the championship points to 7th position as he finished 21st, 41st, and 19th at Michigan, Infineon and Daytona respectively.

Chapter 7
Contract Extension

Dale extended his contract by five years with Hendrick on the 1st of September 2011. This meant that he was going to race up through 2017. He appeared at the chase for sprint cup September 2011 in Chicago for the first time since 2008. He finished 11th at the finale and was 7th in the point standings. He, for the 9th time consecutively, won the most popular driver of the year.

In 2013 he finished 8th in his first race of the season in the Sprint Unlimited, and he qualified for the Budweiser Duel after finishing 11th. After a narrow escape from a car crash, he finished the race securing the 9th position and finished 4th at the DRIVE4COPD 300. He set a new record at Kentucky with a lap time of 29.4 seconds, the speed of 183.6 miles per hour and also won the pole.

While the race was on, Carl Edward beat him to take the lead. After a collision between Denny Hamlin, Dale Earnhardt and Jimmie Johnson, Earnhardt managed a 12th position. Afterwards, at the Coke Zero 400, he edged into the 8th place. He swept the top 10 in the two Daytona races alongside Johnson and Ryan Newman.

The season finale was a tough one as the closing 67 laps were vigorously contested for by Matt Kenseth, Earnhardt and Denny Hamlin. Although Hamlin won, Earnhardt bagged the 3rd position making him among the top 5, which was his first at Homestead. He ended the season with a 5th position, two poles, ten top 5s and a massive 22 top 10 finishes. The 5th of December 2013 saw Earnhardt win the most popular driver for the 11th time consecutively, a record breaker, surpassing Bill Elliot's record of 10 straight awards. Dale's team had their crew chief Steve Letarte leave the pit box to become a member of NASCAR on their broadcast team.

They assured their fans that this move would not affect their winning. Dale would have won the Sprint Unlimited if not for his slight collision with Marcos Ambrose, sending him into the wall and ending the race with a 9th position. He also did poorly in the 1st Budweiser Duel despite starting the race well. He won his second Daytona 500 after struggling with his car. He also finished 2nd at Phoenix.

Dale gambled on not running out of gas at Vegas and ended up in the second position. He started strong at Bristol with an opportunity to be the second driver in history to begin the season with a straight top two for the fourth time until his tires malfunctioned forcing him to finish 24th.

Dale started at the Auto Club Speedway on the 15th position. Unfortunately, he lost his front tire on the 44th lap, hitting the outside wall. After several attempts to salvage the situation, he finished with a 12th position which was enough to help him maintain second place position in point standings. The next week, he battled to remain in the top 5 with a lead of 25 laps, and a 3rd position making it the 4th time he was finishing in the top 3 positions.

He had a crash on the 13th lap leading to a fire outbreak while at Texas. This led him to finish last and dropped to the 5th position in points. He raced the top five and finished 2nd at Darlington. After the Easter break, Dale started strong, leading seven laps before bad breaks set in. He ended up finishing in the seventh position.

At Talladega the next week, he led 26 laps before he lost control of his car leaving him at the 26th position. He finished 5th at Kansas after taking the lead for a few laps and finished 4th at the sprint all-star race. The following week saw him in the top 5 at the Coca-Cola 600 before he fell victim to a pit stop which saw him finish 19th with two laps left. At Dover, he was among the top ten battling for a chance, he got that chance among the top 5 but later lost the track before ending with a 9th position.

At Pocono, Earnhardt capitalized on the Brad Kieslowski and Danica Patrick clash to be victorious the second time at Pocono. This made it the first time he won various races in a season since 2004. At Michigan, he was among the top 5 only to finish 7th. At Sonoma, Earnhardt scored his best road course finishing by remaining relevant in the top ten all through the race and finished 3rd.

He finished 5th the week after at Kentucky. At Daytona, he managed a 14th position after a pile-up of 16 cars. He did better the next week at New Hampshire, finishing 10th and 9th at Indianapolis. The main reason why Steve Letarte was replaced was finally known as Greg Ives, the Nationwide Series crew chief of Chase Elliot, returned to Hendrick to be Dale's Crew chief.

At Pocono, Dale began with a 9th position and was in the top ten for most of the race. With 14 laps left, he took the lead, but Kurt Busch's cut tire ended his domination and forced him to the 9th position. He finished 11th at Glen Watkins and finished 5th at Michigan the next week.

At Richmond, he ended with a 12th place finish and while in the chase grid, he seeded 3rd place. He took the 11th position in the challenger round of the chase. At New Hampshire, he ended with a 9th position and finished

17th at Dover. He ended 5th at Kansas. With this win, he hoped to increase his chances in the championship.

After taking the lead in 45 laps, he ended up in the 39th position after suffering from a cut right tire. This led him to fall to the 11th position. At Charlotte Dale was looking good, but after a shifter failed he ended up in 20th position. At Talladega, Earnhardt started 28th but ended with a 31st position finish which ended his title chase. At Martinsville, after leading 79 laps, he struggled for the lead from the 5th position and kept at it until the end. This was his first ever win at Martinsville.

At Texas, he started 12th and finished 6th, while at Phoenix he finished 8th. At Homestead, he finished 14th. In the final standings, he finished 8th with four wins, 12 top 5s, 20 top 10s and won the most popular driver for the 12th time.

In 2015, he took the 9th position in the Sprint Unlimited. The 19th of February saw him win the Budweiser Duel making it his fourth win in any Budweiser Duel. Daytona 500 saw him lead more than 30 laps only to get all clumsy and fall to the 16th position with less than 15 laps to go. However, he fought his way through to finish 3rd. This made it the 5th time he finished in the top 3 in the Daytona 500 in 6 years. He finished 3rd at Atlanta and 4th at Vegas making him among the top 5.

At Phoenix, he took the last position and finished 6th at Auto Club. At Martinsville because of a crash, he ended in the 36th position. At Texas, he ended up 2nd and at Bristol, he got the 16th position. At Richmond, he ended up 14th position, and at Talladega, he ended up 6th. At Kansas he took the 3rd position, and at Charlotte, he repeated the feat at Kansas and ended up 3rd. However, at Dover, he finished 14th while at Pocono he struggled to earn the 11th place.

At Michigan, he bagged the second position, while at Daytona, he was the pole winner at Coke Zero 400. He won the race itself after struggling to maintain the lead. He became the 23rd driver to lead over 8k laps in the sprint history. At Kentucky, he had issues with his brakes which led to a collision with Danica Patrick of which she acted back. Dale spoke out that he was shocked at her reaction, considering the fact he had not run into her intentionally but as a result of a problem with his brakes. He finished 5th at New Hampshire and 22nd at Indianapolis. He finished 4th at Pocono, 11th at Watkins Glen, and 10th at Michigan, 9th at Bristol and 8th at Darlington.

At Richmond, he finished 5th. This is the 8th time in the chase and he ended up being seeded 6th for the first chase race. He ended up 12th place at Chicagoland but finished 25th at New Hampshire. Dover welcomed him with a 3rd position after struggling through the race. At Charlotte, he ended up 29th, 21st at Kansas, 2nd at Talladega, 4th at Martinsville, 6th at Texas, 3rd at Phoenix and 40th at Homestead. He went on to win the most popular Driver in 2015 for the 13th time.

In 2016, he finished 15th in the sprint unlimited. He won the Can-am duel race, 36th at Daytona, 2nd in Atlanta, 8th at Vegas, 5th at Phoenix, 11th at Fontana, 14th at Martinsville, 2nd at Texas and 2nd at Bristol. He finished

2nd at the Xfinity Series at Richmond, 40th at Talladega, 15th at Kansas and finished 32nd at Dover. He finished 3rd at the All-star Race. In 2017, he finished 37th in Daytona and 5th at Texas. He later announced 2017 as his last year as a full-time driver.

He finished 13th at Richmond, and while at Talladega, he finished 7th. In his last race, he finished 25th and was 21st on the point standing. He ended the season with a one top five, eight top ten's, seven DNFs and two poles. He won the most popular driver award again for the umpteenth time with a record of 15 straight wins. Although Bill Elliot recorded the highest award for the most popular driver 16 times with a straight 10. In 2018, he finished 4th at the fall Xfinity Race.

Thanks for Reading

Hello, this message is from Naven Johnson. I hope that you enjoyed this book and that it has helped your life in some way. It is my intention to create information that readers will find useful and valuable.

I am grateful when people read my books and I am even more grateful when my readers leave a review. Please leave a review that lets me know what you liked about this book so that I can work on improving future books.

Printed in Great Britain
by Amazon